Puddings Galore!

BY RICHARD HUGHES

THE LAVENDER HOUSE

Published by The Lavender House
39 The Street, Brundall, Norwich, Norfolk, England
Telephone 01603 712215
www.thelavenderhouse.co.uk

ISBN No. 0-9547636-1-0

Photography: Eddie Jones

Design and Editing: Peter Russ

Food Preparation: Richard Hughes and Richard Knights

Contributions from Trevor Hughes

Printing: Norwich Colour Print, Drayton, Norwich

Contents

Introduction

"What's for afters?" A chorus that seems to chime from tables up and down the country as men, women and children seem to have more interest in the sweet finale than in any meat and vegetable that's served before.

"If you don't eat your greens then there is no pudding for you." Is there a more fearful threat known to any small child? The obsession for sweet things isn't something we grow out of. How many of the most sophisticated diners sneak a quick peek at the dessert menu? Basing their choice of starter and main course on whether it will be the nursery pudding or the fresh fruit sorbet to close the meal. Just look at the popularity of the old-fashioned sweet shop, from the jars of fluorescent boiled crunchers, to websites offering coconut tobacco, Parma violets and Pink Panther strawberry chocolate: our obsession with the sweeter things in life knows no bounds. As a lad I would always be much more interested in the pud. Bread and butter pudding, treacle sponge, even tinned peaches with evaporated milk. Occasionally we would have a jam tart, marked out into quarters with a thick line of pastry, offering multi-coloured slices of blackcurrant, strawberry and apricot jam, with the favourite lemon curd tucked alongside. I know the French have their wondrous pâtisseries, and maybe you have eaten a memorable Ille Flottaine or a Gâteau Paris Brest, but very few countries and cultures can match us for the range of sweet treats that are embedded in our culture. A raw sponge mix is a taste not forgotten; the biggest treat in any household is to wipe your finger around the bowl, or better still to win the prize of licking the spoon – and before you've even cooked it! A look at the meal's end can tell you everything, from the season, the weather, the pride and effort in one's self. Rice pudding? Straight from the can, or baked slowly, almost luxuriously in the bottom of the oven, topped with freshly grated nutmeg, with the head of the house demanding the thick skin be deposited in his deep bowl. Humble ingredients transformed to the heights!

As the nights draw in you know you can rely on spotted dick, chocolate pudding with chocolate sauce, even a Sussex Pond pud, revealing a pierced cooked lemon in the centre surrounded by its buttery sugary tart liquor. Summer will see the abundance of soft fruits; from the bottom of the garden, a trip to the PYO, a roadside stall with dirt and straw on the freshest of fruit, to a pristine punnet on a supermarket shelf: it matters little as you are tasting English summer sun. A treat that beckoned, when we had spent a day on crouched knees with aching back and straw-pricked hands, would be the hot strawberry pie, topped with heavily sugared pastry made with the last of the day's pick. The first of the rhubarb, a gooseberry fool, a big fat blemished Bramley served with Bird's custard – all these things should be celebrated and cherished. So here lie the serious puds. Not for the faint-hearted, the nervous, those of delicate dispositions, the dieters and the doubters. These are for those who live life to the full, and believe a lot of what you fancy does you good! Don't be shy when it comes to over-producing. Though I've given you portion sizes, they can be taken with a pinch of salt, or an extra ladle of custard! There is little as indulgent as a dish of leftover rhubarb crumble for breakfast: just serve it with a scoop of crème fraîche to assuage the guilt!

With a culinary history that has been much maligned, a country that can lay claim to the summer pudding, Eton Mess, roly poly and Bakewell tart has a tradition that should be celebrated…with seconds!

GOOSEBERRY AND
ROSEMARY FOOL

Gooseberry and Rosemary Fool

The only fools to eat are gooseberry or rhubarb. Both fruits have that extra level of acidity to balance the cream. The addition of rosemary might look trendy but, in truth, the addition of herbs such as bay leaves, lavender, verbena and the like have been used in desserts since medieval times.

Makes 2 portions

Pre-heat the oven to Gas Mark 3/170°C

125 G GOOSEBERRIES	125 ML DOUBLE CREAM
150 G CASTER SUGAR	1 SMALL GLASS WHITE WINE
A LITTLE WATER	SPRIG FRESH ROSEMARY
SMALL PIECE OF ROOT GINGER	

Poach the gooseberries in a little water with 100 g of the sugar, the ginger and the rosemary.

Allow to cool. Remove the ginger and rosemary from the gooseberries.

Whip the cream with the remaining sugar. As it begins to thicken, add the white wine and whisk until stiff.

Place two-thirds of the gooseberries in a pretty glass.

Fold the remaining gooseberries through the cream.

Top the glass with the cream, decorating with a poached gooseberry and a sprig of rosemary.

Serve with Norfolk White Button Biscuits.

Norfolk White Buttons:

100 G BUTTER	250 G SELF RAISING FLOUR
350 G CASTER SUGAR	1 LEVEL TEASPOON GROUND GINGER
1 EGG	

Whisk the butter and sugar until light and fluffy.

Gradually beat in the egg.

Sift the flour and the ginger into the mixture until a fairly firm dough is obtained.

Roll the dough into small balls, and place them onto a greased baking tray.

Bake for 30 minutes until well risen, hollow and very lightly browned.

HONEY AND HERB
ROASTED PEACH

Honey and Herb Roasted Peach

If you wrap these peaches in foil, you can throw them on your barbecue. They make a slightly more upmarket, but no less delicious, dessert than the banana stuffed with Rolos!

Pre-heat the oven to Gas Mark 4/180°C

RIPE PEACHES	CLEAR HONEY
GARDEN HERBS	UNSALTED BUTTER

- Take each peach and brush liberally with softened butter.

- Drizzle on clear honey.

- Sprinkle on a selection of fresh herbs to include rosemary, lavender, a bay leaf, and thyme.

- Place in a hot oven for approximately 15 minutes.

CRANACHAN

Cranachan

A classic from the Highlands, using Scottish raspberries, heather honey and a wee dram. You can, of course, replace the oats with muesli, then you can tell yourself it's healthy eating!

Serves 4 people

225 G CASTER SUGAR	4 TEASPOONS CLEAR HONEY
8 EGG YOLKS	175 G TOASTED OATMEAL
600 ML WHIPPING CREAM	WHISKY TO TASTE

Whisk the egg yolks and the sugar until pale and creamy.

In a separate bowl whisk in the cream until it begins to thicken.

Fold in the honey, the toasted oats and the whisky to taste.

Pour into a terrine or individual moulds and freeze for at least 4 hours until firm.

Allow to stand for 5 minutes at room temperature before serving.

Top with raspberries, toasted oats and honey.

CARAMELISED PINEAPPLE
WITH BUTTERSCOTCH

Caramelised Pineapple with Butterscotch

If only I had a pound for every time I've served this dish. A permanent fixture on our menu when we first began, we used to slice, roast and score the pineapple and sit the ice-cream in the cavity. This is a much flashier presentation – a kind of Salvador Dali dessert.

Serves 4 to 6 people, depending on the size of the pineapple

1 FRESH SUPER SWEET PINEAPPLE	50G SUGAR
50G BUTTER	

your favourite ice-cream (coconut goes particularly well)

- Peel the pineapple, removing all the eyes and the centre core.

- Heat the butter in a heavy pan and add the sugar.

- As it begins to caramelise, add the pineapple slices.

- Colour each slice. Remove the pineapple onto a tray, pour over the residue of the caramel and juices, and place in a moderate oven whilst you make the butterscotch.

Butterscotch:

50G BUTTER	75ML DOUBLE CREAM
100G SUGAR	

- Melt the butter and then add the sugar. Allow to caramelise – you are looking for quite a deep brown to appear.

- When it has reached this stage, slowly pour in the double cream. Take care – the mixture will be very hot and will bubble viciously!

- Whisk to amalgamate.

- Remove the pineapple from the oven, place a scoop of ice-cream in the centre, pour over the hot butterscotch and serve immediately.

RASPBERRY TART, YOGHURT
CHEESECAKE CREAM

Raspberry Tart, Yoghurt Cheesecake Cream

The tartness of the lemon yoghurt provides the perfect foil for the plump, ripe, luscious raspberries and the creamy mascarpone.

Makes 4 individual tarts or one 23 cm tart

1 SWEET PASTRY TART CASE	100 G ICING SUGAR
250 G FRESH RASPBERRIES	100 ML YOGHURT
200 G MASCARPONE	JUICE AND ZEST OF HALF A LEMON

Beat the cheese, the icing sugar, the yoghurt, and the zest and juice of the lemon until smooth.

Pre-bake the pastry case until crisp and golden.

Spread the cheesecake cream on the base of the tart and top with fresh raspberries.

STRAWBERRY SHORTBREAD

Strawberry Shortbread

A spectacular presentation!

Makes 12 biscuits – 4 portions

Pre-heat the oven to Gas Mark 4/180°C

150 G PLAIN FLOUR	50 G ICING SUGAR
150 G SOFT BUTTER	DASH OF GRAND MARNIER OR YOUR FAVOURITE TIPPLE
75 G CORNFLOUR	50 ML DOUBLE CREAM
75 G CASTER SUGAR	150 G STRAWBERRIES
100 G CREAM CHEESE	ICING SUGAR TO DREDGE

- Cream the butter and the sugar.

- Blend in the sifted flours.

- Push together without kneading the mixture.

- Wrap and chill for at least 20 minutes.

- Gently knead the mixture until pliable. Roll out onto a lightly floured surface and cut out the biscuits.

- Mix together the cream cheese and the icing sugar.

- Add your favourite tipple and the cream and mix well.

- Add half the hulled strawberries. Fold in.

- Bake the biscuits on a sheet of parchment for approximately 12 minutes, until the biscuits have just set. Carefully place onto a wire rack to cool.

- Place the strawberry cream onto the biscuits, making sure you leave the tops plain.

- Place on the remaining cut strawberries.

- Dredge each layer with icing sugar, building up to make shortbread stacks.

ETON MESS

Eton Mess

This is so simple, yet one of the great dishes of the English strawberry harvest.

Makes 4 glasses

125 ML WHIPPING CREAM	250 G STRAWBERRIES
100 G ICING SUGAR	3 MERINGUE SHELLS

Mash half of the strawberries with a fork.

Whip the cream and the icing sugar to a soft peak.

Cut the remaining strawberries in half.

Break the meringue into small pieces.

Fold the meringue and the mashed and the halved strawberries through the whipped cream.

Pile into a glass, and top with a strawberry and meringue.

LEMON AND
BLACKCURRANT JELLY

Lemon and Blackcurrant Jelly

Jellies are viewed as classic children's food, although we are now serving all manner of sweet and savoury "wobblers" in the restaurant. Any jelly should have that just-set texture, and melt as it enters the mouth.

Serves 4

250 G FRESH BLACKCURRANTS	10 LAVENDER FLOWERS (FIND THEM AT GARDEN CENTRES)
75 G GRANULATED SUGAR	8 THICK SLICES OF BRIOCHE TO SERVE (OPTIONAL)

- Gently cook 200 g of the blackcurrants with the sugar and lavender flowers in a saucepan, stirring occasionally until the blackcurrants are thick and syrupy.

- Add the remaining blackcurrants, and chill.

Lemon Jelly:

250 ML LEMON JUICE (ABOUT 6 LEMONS)
125 ML STOCK SYRUP (125 G GRANULATED OR CASTER SUGAR DISSOLVED IN 125 ML WATER THEN SIMMERED FOR 5 MINS)
2 LEAVES GELATINE, SOFTENED IN COLD WATER

- Bring the lemon juice and stock syrup to a boil, stirring occasionally.

- Add the gelatine then strain and leave to cool and set in the fridge.

To serve, spoon some lemon jelly into the base of a Martini glass until one-third full. Add some compote to fill just over half of the glass. Serve with slices of toasted brioche, if you like.

A MOST UNUSUAL
PEACH MELBA

A Most Unusual Peach Melba

I know, I know…you shouldn't mess with the classics, but I'm sure Dame Nelly wouldn't mind. We've simply changed it, using vanilla custard instead of raspberry sauce, raspberry sorbet instead of vanilla ice-cream and, of course, fresh peaches instead of tinned – although they are just as delicious!

Serves 4 people

4 FRESH PEACHES   RASPBERRY SORBET

GRANULATED SUGAR   A FEW RASPBERRIES

PEACH PURÉE
(FLESH FROM 1 PEACH, WHIZZED UP WITH A TOUCH OF ICING SUGAR
AND A LITTLE PEACH SCHNAPPS)

Split and stone the peaches, sprinkle with sugar and glaze under a fierce grill until caramelised.

Allow to cool.

Top with a scoop of raspberry sorbet, and serve with vanilla custard and peach purée.

Custard Sauce:

4 EGG YOLKS   1 VANILLA POD

50 G SUGAR   25 ML COGNAC

100 ML DOUBLE CREAM

Bring the cream to the boil with the vanilla pod and simmer for 5 minutes to infuse. Remove the pod.

Whisk the egg yolks and sugar.

Pour on the hot cream.

Return to the heat, stirring continuously. Do not allow the custard to boil.

When it starts to thicken, remove from the heat and pour in the Cognac.

SUMMER BERRY
MILLE FEUILLE

Summer Berry Mille Feuille

Don't try to pick this up, even I couldn't fit it in my mouth in one go!

Pre-heat the oven to Gas Mark 4/180°C

PUFF PASTRY	WHIPPING CREAM
ICING SUGAR	GRAND MARNIER
SUMMER BERRIES	FRESH MINT

- Pin out the puff pastry as thinly as possible.

- Cut into neat rectangles. Allow to rest. Place on a baking sheet.

- Cover with a silk mat, a sheet of "Bake O Glide" or a sheet of greaseproof paper. Place another baking sheet on top to weigh the pastry down.

- Bake for 15 minutes. Remove the top tray. Allow the pastry to cool.

- Mix the cream with a little sugar, chopped mint and the Grand Marnier.

- Whip the cream to a soft peak.

- Pass some of the berries through a sieve, and sweeten with the sugar to make a little sauce.

- Pick over the fruits, slicing the larger berries.

- Layer the pastry sheets with the berries.

- Spoon over the cream and the puréed sauce.

- Repeat with a second layer.

- Dust the pastry top liberally with icing sugar.

- Using a hot bar or needle, scorch the sugar on the final pastry decoratively.

- Top the mille feuille.

PIMMS JELLY

A terrific picnic dessert, or ideal if you are shut indoors watching the tennis on TV.

Serves 6-8

3 SHEETS LEAF GELATINE

400 ML LEMONADE

175 ML PIMMS NO 1 CUP

JUICE OF ½ LEMON

JUICE OF ½ LIME

284 ML DOUBLE CREAM

2 TABLESPOONS CASTER SUGAR

3 ORANGES (2 PEELED AND SEGMENTED, 1 ZESTED)

250 G STRAWBERRIES (STALKS PULLED OUT)

MINT SPRIGS TO DECORATE

Soak the gelatine in cold water until soft (it will take about 2 minutes).

Heat half the lemonade until just about boiling and remove from the heat.

Lift the gelatine out of the water and stir into the lemonade until dissolved.

Add the Pimms, lemon and lime juice, and remaining lemonade.

Pour through a sieve into a bowl and refrigerate until set.

Lightly whip the cream and stir in the sugar and orange zest.

Slice the strawberries and stir half of them through the set jelly.

To serve, spoon some jelly into a glass then add more strawberries and some orange segments. Finish with a blob of the orange cream, a sprig of mint and, if you like, a strip of zest.

AUTUMN FRUITS
IN RED WINE

Autumn Fruits in Red Wine

A bowl of late summer sun, served simply, to be enjoyed at its peak.

250 G BLACKBERRIES, RASPBERRIES, BLACKCURRANTS, CHERRIES	ZEST AND JUICE OF AN ORANGE
125 ML LIGHT RED WINE (SUCH AS A BEAUJOLAIS)	1 SMALL CINNAMON STICK
100 G SUGAR	CRÈME FRAÎCHE, ICE-CREAM, MASCARPONE OR CLOTTED CREAM
125 ML WATER	

- Bring the water, sugar, cinnamon and juice of the orange to the boil.

- Simmer for 5 minutes.

- Add the red wine and the fruits, and return to a gentle boil.

- Turn off the heat and allow to cool in the syrup.

- Place in a deep bowl and serve with a scoop of your chosen accompaniment.

PASSION FRUIT
MERINGUES

Passion Fruit Meringues

So many of the exotic fruits – carambola, kiwi, papaya and the like – are absolutely tasteless. The passion fruit is the exception however: the ugly little devils release the most beautiful aroma that will perfume the whole dish. Remember, the more wrinkled the better!

Makes 12 meringues

Pre-heat the oven to Gas Mark ½/130°C

4 EGG WHITES	PINCH OF SALT
225 G CASTER SUGAR	

Place the egg whites and the pinch of salt into a spotlessly clean bowl.

Add half the caster sugar and whisk to a soft peak.

Add the remainder of the sugar and continue to whisk.

The meringue should be stiff enough to turn upside down and remain in the bowl.

Pipe the meringue onto greased baking parchment into a circle 8 cm in diameter with a raised edge, to form a nest. Bake for 2 hours, until the meringue is crisp and dry.

Turn off the oven and leave in the oven until the meringue is cool. When cooled, carefully remove from the paper.

The Filling:

300 ML DOUBLE CREAM	**3** PASSION FRUIT
100 G ICING SUGAR	**25** ML GRAND MARNIER

1 passion fruit to decorate

Whip the double cream lightly.

Add the icing sugar, and the Grand Marnier.

Add the pulp from the passion fruit and fold in.

Spoon the cream into the centre of the cooked meringue.

Pile on the pulp from another passion fruit and dust with icing sugar.

PINEAPPLE, FENNEL AND
STRAWBERRY GAZPACHO

Pineapple, Fennel and Strawberry Gazpacho

This can be made in seconds, and is a favourite in our "nine course tasting menus". People ask for the ingredients, expecting it be compiled of all sorts of things. I'm sure that they don't believe me when I give them the recipe! It can't be that simple – can it?

Makes 6 shot glasses

1 SMALL RIPE SWEET PINEAPPLE	200 G FRESH STRAWBERRIES
200 G SMALL FRESH FENNEL	JUICE AND ZEST OF 1 SMALL LIME
HANDFUL OF FENNEL FROND TOPS	50 G SUGAR

In a food processor blitz the pineapple, the fennel and the fennel tops.

Spoon into a glass.

Place the strawberries in the food processor with the lime and the sugar, blitz and top up the glasses.

STRAWBERRIES WITH ORANGE, VANILLA
AND PEPPERCORN CARAMEL

Strawberries with Orange, Vanilla and Peppercorn Caramel

In the late 1970s, before snail porridge, bacon ice-cream and tobacco syrup, Robert Carrier was serving this at Hintlesham Hall. At the time the combination of strawberries and peppercorns was daring in the extreme!

Makes 4 portions

400 G FRESH ENGLISH STRAWBERRIES

250 G GRANULATED SUGAR

JUICE AND ZEST OF 1 ORANGE

HALF A SPLIT VANILLA POD

16 GREEN PEPPERCORNS

Stalk and wash the strawberries and cut in half.

Place the sugar in a heavy-bottomed saucepan and cover with cold water.

Place on the heat and bring to the boil.

When it comes to the boil, reduce the heat and simmer until the sugar begins to caramelise.

Remove from the heat and pour in the juice and zest from the orange, the vanilla pod and the peppercorns.

Allow the syrup to cool.

Place the strawberries in a pretty dish and spoon over the syrup, ensuring the peppercorns are equally divided between the portions.

FRUIT SORBETS

Fruit Sorbets

So often people look forward to the dessert, but then just can't manage it. They often opt for a sorbet, yet freshly made, it needn't be the sorry option. We don't have such a thing as an ice-cream or sorbet maker, we simply make the mixture, freeze it, then feed it into the food processor to smash up the ice crystals and incorporate the air. It sounds Neanderthal, but it makes some of the smoothest sorbets I've ever tasted.

500 G FRESH FRUIT	JUICE AND ZEST OF 1 LEMON
500 ML WATER	1 GLASS OF WHITE WINE (OPTIONAL)
500 G GRANULATED SUGAR	

- Bring the water, lemon juice and zest, and sugar to the boil. Allow to cool.

- Add the white wine if using.

- Pass the fruit through a blender. Sieve.

- Mix the fruit with the stock syrup.

- Place in a freezer.

- When almost frozen, pass through a food processor to break up the crystals and incorporate air into the mixture.

- Return to the freezer for at least 2 hours.

GRILLED GRAPEFRUIT
WITH SHERRY

Grilled Grapefruit with Sherry

A dessert that's equally at home as a starter, or even for breakfast if you've had a particularly heavy night before!

Makes 2 portions

2 PINK GRAPEFRUIT

1 GLASS SWEET SHERRY

2 EGG YOLKS

50 G CASTER SUGAR

1 DESSERTSPOON BOILING WATER

Segment the grapefruit, ensuring the fruit is free of all pith and skin.

Place the fruit in an ovenproof dish.

Put the egg yolks, the sherry and the sugar into a bowl.

Using an electric whisk, beat to mix.

Add the spoonful of boiling water and continue to whisk until the mixture goes light and frothy, mixing until it's cold.

Pour over the grapefruit segments and place under a grill to colour.

Serve immediately.

BITTERSWEET
CHOCOLATE POTS

Bittersweet Chocolate Pots

A simple presentation, but it's the classic dessert that appears in all French bistros, following the onion soup and steak with Roquefort and frites.

Makes 6 individual pots

Pre-heat the oven to Gas Mark 3/170°C

100 ML MILK	175 ML DOUBLE CREAM
140 G DARK BITTER CHOCOLATE (AT LEAST 65% COCOA SOLIDS)	3 LARGE EGG YOLKS
1 VANILLA POD, SPLIT	75 G SUGAR

- Bring the milk, cream, the vanilla pod and chocolate to a simmer.

- Stir until the chocolate has dissolved. Allow to cool.

- Whisk the egg yolks and the sugar.

- Fold into the chocolate mixture.

- Pour into ramekins, coffee cups or other suitable little pots.

- Place the pots into a deep tray, filling the tray with hot water until it reaches halfway up the sides of the chocolate pots.

- Place in the oven and bake for 30-35 minutes until the custards are just set.

- Allow to cool and serve in the pots.

CHOCOLATE FONDANT

Chocolate Fondant

Years ago I produced this for a prestigious national chef's competition, only to be told by the judge that I'd lost marks because the centre wasn't cooked! Oh well, you can't win them all!

Pre-heat the oven to Gas Mark 5/190°C

175G DARK CHOCOLATE (MIN. 50% COCOA SOLIDS)

80G UNSALTED BUTTER

4 EGG YOLKS

3 WHOLE EGGS

75G CASTER SUGAR

75G PLAIN FLOUR

1 DESSERTSPOON COCOA POWDER

Place the eggs, the egg yolks and the sugar in a bowl.

Whisk over a pan of hot water.

Whisk until white, creamy and double in volume.

Over another pan of hot water, slowly melt the butter and the chocolate.

Sift the cocoa and the flour.

Pour the chocolate mixture onto the whisked egg yolks.

Carefully amalgamate the two mixtures.

Gently fold the flour and cocoa into the mixture.

Butter a suitable individual mould and dust inside with a flour/cocoa mixture.

Gently spoon in the chocolate mixture until the mould is three-quarters full.

Chill for at least 4 hours. Overnight if possible.

Bake for 8 minutes.

Gently turn out. The mixture should still be liquid but hot inside, almost like a chocolate sponge with the sauce inside.

SOFT CHOCOLATE AND
ALMOND BUTTER CAKES

Soft Chocolate and Almond Butter Cakes

The most moreish chocolate cakes we've ever made.

Makes 6 individual cakes

Pre-heat the oven to Gas Mark 4/180°C

85G UNSALTED BUTTER	75G GROUND ALMONDS
85G DARK CHOCOLATE	1 TABLESPOON MILD HONEY
170G SIFTED ICING SUGAR	3 LARGE EGG WHITES, LIGHTLY BEATEN
45G PLAIN FLOUR	

- Prepare the brown butter: in a small saucepan heat the butter over a moderately high heat. The butter will go through several stages: after 3 to 4 minutes it will begin to brown, with a nutty aroma. When it reaches this stage remove it from the heat and transfer to a large bowl to stop the cooking. Set aside to cool.

- Gently melt the chocolate.

- Blend the icing sugar, the flour and the almonds.

- Beat in the chocolate.

- Beat in the egg whites and the honey. Beat well.

- Add the butter and mix to blend.

- Well butter the individual ramekins or suitable moulds.

- Pour in the batter and chill for approximately 30 minutes, allowing the batter to firm up.

- Cook the cakes for approximately 15 minutes. The cakes should be slightly undercooked in the centre.

- Turn out onto a wire rack and cool.

BAKED CHOCOLATE TART

Baked Chocolate Tart

We have a 'Chef for a Day' cookery experience at the restaurant when customers can spend the day in the kitchen, cooking for their friends who will turn up for dinner to enjoy the fruits of the day's labour. Strangely, the participants are almost always men and most of them plump for this delicious tart as their dessert.

Serves 6-8 people

1 loose-bottomed 21 cm tart or 4 individual 8 cm tartlet tins

Pre-heat the oven to Gas Mark 3/170°C

Pastry:

225 G PLAIN FLOUR	25 G ICING SUGAR
PINCH OF SALT	1 EGG YOLK
140 G BUTTER	COLD WATER TO BIND

Blend the flour, salt, butter and sugar in a food processor for a few seconds.

Add enough water to bind it together.

Turn the pastry out onto a floured surface. Mould the pastry together with your hands, wrap in cling film and chill for 30 minutes.

Knead the pastry gently and line the chosen tart tin.

Bake the pastry case, using baking beans, until it has just set (about 10 minutes).

Remove the baking beans.

Brush the inside of the pastry case with a little beaten egg white and return to the oven for 2 minutes.

Filling:

400 G DARK CHOCOLATE (MIN. 50% COCOA SOLIDS)	250 ML DOUBLE CREAM
150 ML MILK	2 FREE-RANGE EGGS

Place the chocolate in a saucepan with the cream and milk.

Bring slowly to a simmer, stirring continuously. Whisk until all the chocolate has melted.

Beat the eggs in a separate bowl. Pour on the chocolate mixture.

Place the pastry case in the oven, and pour in the chocolate mixture until it's almost flush to the top.

Bake for approximately 35 minutes until the chocolate filling has just set.

Remove from the oven.

Allow to cool before removing from the tin.

Serve with a scoop of mascarpone for extra richness!

GROWN UP BROWNIES

Grown Up Brownies

For years I couldn't get the hang of baking brownies: they always seemed to be soft and squidgy in the middle, until it dawned on me…they're supposed to be like that ! These are very rich and a real treat for tea-time or with double cream as a sophisticated pud.

Makes 12-16 brownies

Pre-heat the oven to Gas Mark 5/190°C

350 G DARK CHOCOLATE, NOT LESS THAN 50% COCOA SOLIDS	75 G SELF RAISING FLOUR
225 G BUTTER	100 G WALNUTS, BROKEN
2 TEASPOONS INSTANT COFFEE	100 G CHOPPED PRUNES
1 TABLESPOON HOT WATER	200 G CHOPPED CHOCOLATE PIECES
3 LARGE EGGS	1 SMALL GLASS OF BRANDY
225 G CASTER SUGAR	

- Melt the 350 g of chocolate and the butter in a bowl over a pan of hot water.
- Soak the prunes in the cognac.
- Dissolve the coffee powder with the hot water.
- In a separate bowl mix the coffee, the eggs and the sugar.
- Gradually beat in the chocolate mixture to the egg sugar mixture.
- Fold in the flour, the prunes, the walnuts, the cognac and the chopped chocolate.
- Pour the mixture into the prepared tin.
- Bake for 45 minutes.
- Leave to cool in the tin, then cut into generous squares.

BAILEYS WHITE
CHOCOLATE CHEESECAKE

Baileys & White Chocolate Cheesecake

I'd never been a fan of cheesecakes, remembering the sickly chewy bars topped with tinned fruit, tinged with gelatine, that frequented the sweet trolleys of the late 1970s. This is an altogether different prospect, with the soft cheese just set by the chocolate.

Makes one 23 cm cheesecake – or approximately 4 individuals

225 G CHOCOLATE CHIP COOKIES

50 G BUTTER

225 G MASCARPONE

100 G WHITE CHOCOLATE, GENTLY MELTED

25 G CASTER SUGAR

300 ML DOUBLE CREAM

125 ML BAILEYS

Crush the biscuits in a food processor, or in a bag with a rolling pin.

Gently melt the butter and mix in the biscuit crumbs.

Stir and then press into the base of a 23 cm (9 inch) spring-loaded cake tin.

Beat the mascarpone and the sugar until smooth.

Stir in the melted chocolate and the Baileys.

Fold in the whipped cream.

Spoon on to the biscuit base.

Smooth and allow to chill for at least 4 hours before serving.

COFFEE CREAM CUPS

Coffee Cream Cups

Very rich, so you won't need too much for the desired impact!
A fun presentation – serve it with chocolate fudge.

Makes 6 small coffee cups

170 G CASTER SUGAR	2 HEAPED TEASPOONS GOOD QUALITY INSTANT COFFEE GRANULES
225 G MASCARPONE	2 LEAVES GELATINE
400 ML WHIPPING CREAM	

- Dissolve the coffee in a minimum of hot water.

- Soak the leaf gelatine in cold water.

- Bring the cream to the boil.

- Whisk in the coffee.

- Squeeze the water from the gelatine, and stir the gelatine into the cream.

- Remove from the heat.

- Whisk in the sugar.

- Allow to cool slightly then whisk in the mascarpone.

- Pour into coffee cups and chill for at least 4 hours.

Lavender Crème Brûlée

Lavender Crème Brûlée

When customers visit The Lavender House for the first time they expect it to be decorated in lavender, with the theme recurring through the menu. Though one of my favourite culinary flowers, this is one of the few times you'll find it on the menu. The flavour should be delicate, so don't be tempted to overdo it.

Makes 6 ramekins

Pre-heat the oven to Gas Mark 3/170°C

6 EGG YOLKS	**100** G CASTER SUGAR
125 ML SINGLE CREAM	**¹/₂** TEASPOON DRIED LAVENDER FLOWERS

Pound the lavender flowers with a pestle and mortar.

Place into the cream and bring to a gentle simmer.

Remove from the heat and allow to infuse for at least 10 minutes. Strain.

Whisk the egg yolks and the sugar.

Pour on the cream.

Place into ramekins or other suitable moulds.

Place the ramekins into a deep tray, pouring hot water into the tray until it reaches approximately halfway up the sides of the ramekin.

Place in the oven and cook until the custards have just set: this should take approximately 30 minutes.

Allow the custards to cool, sprinkle the top with caster sugar and caramelise under a fierce grill or with a blowtorch.

Allow the sugar to cool before serving.

CRÊPES SUZETTE

Crêpes Suzette

This was a "must-have" Saturday night dessert at all classy restaurants in the late 1960s and 1970s. The previous owners of our restaurant were still performing with the gueridon lamp, cooking and flaming at the table every weekend until we banished the trolley to the garage. Having served this at a recent retro night, perhaps we may have been a tad hasty!

Makes enough pancakes for 4 people

The Pancakes:

125 G PLAIN FLOUR	PINCH OF SALT
1 LARGE EGG	65 ML MILK

Whisk the sifted flour and salt with the egg and milk to make a smooth batter.

Strain and allow to stand for 20 minutes.

Fry in a cast flat pan using a little butter between each pancake.

Stack the pancakes, using a strip of greaseproof paper in between each one.

The Syrup:

JUICE AND ZEST OF 1 ORANGE	50 G BUTTER
SPLASH OF GRAND MARNIER	100 G LIGHT BROWN SUGAR

Melt the butter and the sugar until it just starts to caramelise.

Add the Grand Marnier, tipping gently into the flame to burn off the alcohol and create a spectacle!

Add the juice and zest of the orange.

Boil to a syrupy consistency.

Return the pancakes to the syrup and serve immediately.

CRÈME CARAMELS

When I first started work in the late 1970s, this was the only dessert I could make with any modicum of success. That is an indication of how simple they are. Take care when turning them out – they are very light and quite delicate.

Makes 8 caramels

Pre-heat the oven to Gas Mark 3/170°C

150 G GRANULATED SUGAR	100 G SUGAR
½ TEASPOON GLUCOSE SYRUP	450 ML SINGLE CREAM
WATER	VANILLA POD OR ESSENCE
ZEST OF 1 LARGE ORANGE	1 SHERRY GLASS MEASURE OF GRAND MARNIER
4 EGGS	

Place the granulated sugar in a heavy bottomed saucepan.

Add just enough water to cover the sugar and slowly bring to the boil.

Add the glucose syrup and return to a steady boil. Do not stir.

Simmer the sugar until it begins to caramelise, then watch it like a hawk!

When it turns a deep golden colour drop in the orange zest and remove from the heat.

Plunge the pan into a bowl of cold water to stop the cooking and colouring.

Pour the caramel, with some of the zest, into your chosen mould.

Bring the cream to the boil with the vanilla.

Let it simmer for five minutes.

Remove the vanilla pod, scraping the seeds into the cream.

Whisk the eggs with the sugar and pour on the cream.

Add the Grand Marnier.

Pour the custard into the cold moulds.

Cook in a water bath (as for the crème brûlée).

The custard should be just set – this will take approximately 45 minutes.

Remove from the oven and allow to cool in the water bath.

To serve, carefully loosen around the base of the custard with your fingers, then gently ease out onto the serving dish.

CHERRY TRIFLES

Cherry Trifles

We buy big jars of these French cherries. They are sensational – expensive, but worth every penny. They are placed just inside our walk-in fridge, and many is the time I've been caught with fingers in the jar – guilty as sin!

125 G SPONGE CAKE	1 WHOLE EGG
50 G GRIOTTINE CHERRIES SOAKED IN KIRSCH	2 EGG YOLKS
200 ML MILK	125 ML WHIPPING CREAM
1 VANILLA POD	50 G SUGAR
40 G SUGAR	TOASTED FLAKED ALMONDS
25 G PLAIN FLOUR	

- Heat the milk with the vanilla pod.

- Whisk the egg yolks, whole egg, sugar and flour.

- Remove the pod from the milk.

- Pour the milk onto the egg mixture, stirring continuously.

- Return to the heat.

- Bring to the boil, stirring continuously.

- Allow to cool.

- Place the sponge in the base of a pretty glass.

- Spoon over the syrup from the cherries then add a generous portion of cherries.

- Pipe in the cold custard.

- Whip the cream with the sugar and a little more of the syrup from the cherries.

- Pipe onto the custard.

- Top with a few toasted flaked almonds.

BANOFFEE PIE

Banoffee Pie

This is the best thing I've ever eaten. I used to work in a Michelin starred country house in the early 1980s and this was always on the menu. However, we told no-one that we made the filling with condensed milk. You can, of course, buy dulche de leche instead of the tinned milk, but somehow it just doesn't taste the same. Boil more than one tin at a time, and keep them in the cupboard for when you need them.

Makes one 23 cm tart or 4 individual tarts

1 PASTRY CASE, BAKED UNTIL CRISP AND GOLDEN	150 ML DOUBLE CREAM
1 SMALL TIN CONDENSED MILK	1 TEASPOON INSTANT COFFEE
2 BANANAS	50 G ICING SUGAR

The day before you make it, boil the tin of condensed milk for at least 4 hours, ensuring that the water is always kept topped up, then allow the tin to cool in the water.

Open the tin and spread the milk, which should have transformed into a magical creamy toffee, onto the base of the pastry case.

Mash the bananas with the icing sugar and a squeeze of lemon. Spread onto the toffee.

Whip the cream.

Dilute the coffee with a minimum of hot water, whisk into the cream with 50g icing sugar.

Pipe onto the top of the pie.

COCONUT BRANDY SNAPS

Coconut Brandy Snaps

Richard Knights in the pastry section is an absolute perfectionist, cutting each snap with a cutter to ensure a perfect circle. Many's the Saturday evening when we've feasted on all the off-cuts for our tea!

Makes enough snaps for 4 people

Pre-heat the oven to Gas Mark 5/190°C

100 G BUTTER	150 ML DOUBLE CREAM
100 G GRANULATED SUGAR	500 G ICING SUGAR
100 G FLOUR	2 CAPS OF MALIBU
140 G GOLDEN SYRUP	25 G DESICCATED COCONUT, TOASTED

- Melt the butter with the sugar on a low heat.

- Add the flour and stir in. Cook for a minute or so, stirring continuously.

- Add the golden syrup and beat in.

- Allow to cool.

- On a lightly oiled tray or silpat mat, place walnut sized pieces of the snap mix, allowing plenty of room for the mixture to spread.

- Bake for approximately 12 minutes until golden.

- Remove from the oven and allow to stand for a few minutes, then carefully lift off the tray with a palette knife and wrap around a cream horn mould.

- Allow to cool completely.

- Whisk the cream with icing sugar until thickened.

- Fold in the Malibu and the toasted coconut.

- Pipe into the cornets.

STEWED PRUNES
AND CUSTARD

E.M. Forster damns the breakfast cry of "Porridge or Prunes" as "the forces that drag English food into the dirt". Describing his return to his homeland on a boat train arriving via Tilbury he sighs "Everything was grey. The porridge was in pallid grey lumps, the prunes swam in grey juice like the wrinkled skulls of old men, grey mist against the grey windows." Perhaps if he feasted on stewed prunes and custard of this ilk, it would have been a happier homecoming!

Makes 2 portions

12 AGEN PRUNES	6 GREEN PEPPERCORNS
ZEST OF SMALL ORANGE AND LEMON	1 BAY LEAF
125 G CASTER SUGAR	SMALL BUNCH OF FRESH LEMON THYME
CINNAMON STICK	125 ML WATER
STAR ANISE	

Place all the ingredients in a saucepan.

Bring to the boil and simmer for 5 minutes.

Allow to cool and serve with the custard.

Custard:

4 EGG YOLKS	1 VANILLA POD
50 G SUGAR	25 ML COGNAC
100 ML DOUBLE CREAM	

Bring the cream to the boil with the vanilla pod and simmer for 5 minutes to infuse. Remove the pod.

Whisk the egg yolks and sugar.

Pour on the hot cream.

Return to the heat, stirring continuously. Do not allow the custard to boil.

When it starts to thicken, remove from the heat and pour in the Cognac.

Spoon the prunes into a deep bowl, and pour on the custard.

SWEET PLUM OMELETTE

Sweet Plum Omelette

I don't think I've ever seen a sweet omelette on anybody's menu, except a few diners in the United States. A pity, because they are really something special when eaten straight from the pan.

For each omelette:

3 FREE RANGE EGGS	50 G RIPE PLUMS
ICING SUGAR	25 G CASTER SUGAR
50 G BUTTER	TOUCH OF WATER

- Gently stew the plums in a little water with the caster sugar.

- Separate two of the eggs, whisking the whites.

- Whisk together the whole egg and the two egg yolks with a teaspoon of icing sugar.

- Fold in the whisked egg whites.

- Heat an omelette pan, adding the knob of butter, until it begins to froth.

- Pour in the egg mixture, stirring lightly with a fork until it just begins to set.

- Gently fold the omelette over.

- Liberally dust with icing sugar, and place under a grill or mark with a hot bar.

- Serve with the plums.

PRUNE AND
ALMOND TART

Prune and Almond Tart

This is a personal favourite of mine, much beloved by the French, but none the worse for that! If you get the chance to soak the prunes in some Armagnac it will be even better!

Makes one 8" tart

Pre-heat the oven to Gas Mark 5/190°C

Sweet Pastry:

400 G PLAIN FLOUR	1 EGG
200 G BUTTER	50 G ICING SUGAR

Combine in a food processor.

Filling:

150 G PITTED PRUNES, SOAKED IN COGNAC

Frangipani:

200 G CASTER SUGAR	3 MEDIUM EGGS
200 G BUTTER	200 G GROUND ALMONDS

marmalade for the base

Cream the butter and the sugar until light and fluffy.

Fold in the egg and the ground almonds, a little at a time, alternately.

Line the flan ring or tartlet case.

Cover the base sparingly with the marmalade.

Pipe or spoon in the frangipani.

Place on the prunes decoratively.

Bake for approximately 45 minutes. Cover if necessary to ensure the base is cooked.

HONEYCOMB SUNDAE

Honeycomb Sundae

To turn this honeycomb into a memorable sundae, take your favourite vanilla ice-cream, remove from the container, put into a bowl and allow it to soften slightly. Fold in the broken honeycomb. Alternatively, to make a home-made version of a Crunchie bar, simply dip the honeycomb into melted chocolate.

500 G GRANULATED SUGAR	JUICE OF ½ LEMON
250 ML WATER	**1** TEASPOON BICARBONATE OF SODA

- Clean out a heavy saucepan, rubbing the inside with lemon to ensure it's spotlessly clean.

- Place in the sugar and water and slowly bring to the boil.

- Increase the heat and cook until it reaches a golden caramel colour.

- Remove from the heat, and squeeze in the lemon and sift in the bicarbonate of soda (take care as this mixture will quite literally erupt).

- Pour straight into an oiled tray and allow to set.

- Simply break up into bite-sized chunks.

RAISIN AND RICOTTA
DROP CAKES

We always make these when we visit primary schools. Very quick to make, you can serve them for breakfast or as a dessert. If you top them with honey, maple syrup or, dare I suggest it, golden syrup, they become irresistible!

Serves 6

350 G RICOTTA

185 ML MILK

4 EGGS, SEPARATED

140 G PLAIN FLOUR

1 TEASPOON BAKING POWDER

BUTTER FOR FRYING

150 G RAISINS

PLAIN YOGHURT AND MAPLE SYRUP TO SERVE

ICING SUGAR TO DUST

Mix the ricotta, milk and egg yolks in a bowl.

Sift the flour, baking powder and a pinch of salt into a bowl.

Add to the ricotta mixture and mix.

Whisk the egg whites in a clean dry bowl until stiff peaks form.

Using a large metal spoon, fold the egg whites through the batter in 2 batches.

Lightly butter a large non-stick frying pan and drop 2 tablespoons of batter per drop cake in the pan (don't cook more than three per batch).

Scatter 6-8 raisins over each drop cake, and cook over a low-medium heat for 2 minutes or until the drop cakes have golden undersides.

Turn and cook on the other side until golden and cooked through.

Stack three drop cakes on each plate, top with yoghurt and maple syrup, and dust with icing sugar.

FLAPJACKS

Flapjacks

Can we class flapjacks as a pudding? Well they are the mainstay of "pack ups" from children's lunchboxes to workers on the land, so they get my vote! The big advantage is that you can make a load of them and store them in a tin for whenever you're peckish.

Makes 16 flapjacks, using a 30 cm × 23 cm tin

Pre-heat the oven to Gas Mark 3/170°C

225 G BUTTER	175 G MUESLI
225 G DEMERARA SUGAR	100 G OATS
2 TABLESPOONS GOLDEN SYRUP	

- Melt the butter with the sugar and the syrup.

- Stir in the muesli and the oats. Mix well.

- Turn into the tray. Bake for 30 minutes and leave to cool in the tin for at least 10 minutes before cutting into bars.

TREACLE LOAF

Treacle Loaf

I've always eaten this hot, though I'm sure it's equally good cold. The aromas emanating from the oven, then as it sits on the cooling wire, will be tempting enough to ensure you do the same!

Makes 12 squares

Pre-heat the oven to Gas Mark 3/170°C

100G BUTTER	225G SELF RAISING FLOUR
100G SOFT BROWN SUGAR	1 TEASPOON GROUND GINGER
2 EGGS	1 TEASPOON MIXED SPICE
150G BLACK TREACLE	2 TABLESPOONS MILK
150G GOLDEN SYRUP	50G WALNUTS (OPTIONAL)

Line an 18cm square cake tin with buttered greaseproof.

Whisk together the softened butter, sugar, eggs, walnuts, treacle and syrup.

Sift the flour and the spices, and fold into the treacle mixture.

Stir in the milk.

Pour into the prepared tin.

Bake for 70 minutes until well risen and firm to the touch.

Remove from the oven and place on a cooling rack.

BAKED APPLE WITH
MARZIPAN AND WALNUTS

Baked Apple with Marzipan and Walnuts

This is a lovely dessert to make when you're in a hurry. The filling gives it a nice festive feel, so it's ideal for Boxing Day lunch when you've returned from that breezy stroll along the beach!

Serves 4

Pre-heat the oven to Gas Mark 4/180°C

4 MEDIUM SIZED BRAMLEY APPLES, FREE FROM BRUISING	**50**G RAISINS
50G MARZIPAN	**50**G SOFT BROWN SUGAR
50G WALNUTS	**50**G BUTTER

- Carefully remove the centres of the apples with an apple corer.

- Make a small incision around the centre of the apple to ensure that the skin doesn't split and cause the apple to burst.

- Mix the remaining ingredients together, and pack into the cavities in the centre of the apple.

- Place in a dish and bake for 20 minutes.

- Serve with cream or custard.

APPLE AND DATE
CHARLOTTE

Is there anything more satisfying than producing an acclaimed plateful from a few humble store cupboard ingredients? The finest rice pudding, thrown together with a few pennies worth of rice, a splash of double cream, a dessertspoon of sugar and a good slug of rum, or how about a lovely crumble with rhubarb from the garden and a pinch of ginger. From a few bruised Bramleys, stale bread and butter, I give you this beautiful dish.

Makes 4 individual portions

Pre-heat the oven to Gas Mark 5/190°C

4 LARGE BRAMLEY APPLES	JUICE AND ZEST OF 1 LEMON
8 MEDJOOL DATES (OPTIONAL)	125 G UNSALTED BUTTER
175 G CASTER SUGAR	12 SLICES SLICED WHITE BREAD
1 TEASPOON CINNAMON	

Peel and core the apples.

Chop up, alongside the dates.

Place the apples, dates and the juice and zest of the lemon in a saucepan with 50 g of the butter and 125 g of the sugar. Add the cinnamon.

Simmer gently until the apple begins to break down.

Meanwhile liberally brush the insides of four dariole moulds with the remainder of the butter, and coat with the remainder of the sugar.

Cut eight discs of bread using an appropriate cutter.

Place one in the base of each mould.

Cut the remaining bread into panels.

Line the moulds, slightly overlapping each piece of bread.

Pack in the apple and date mixture.

Fold over the panels of bread.

Top with the remaining discs of bread, ensuring they have been liberally buttered and sugared.

Bake for 20 minutes.

Turn out and serve with vanilla ice-cream, clotted cream or, for the true English person, lashings of custard!

APPLE MERINGUE PIE

Apple Meringue Pie

It was always a thrill whenever we had lemon meringue pie, though it was one of the few times that Mum would use a packet mix for 'afters'. I preferred it straight from the oven – when the lemon filling was cut and served it would spread all over the dish and tablecloth. This is a simple version. If you use Bramleys it can be just as tart as using lemon or lime – you need something to offset the sweet meringue.

Serves 6-8 people

1 loose-bottomed 21 cm tart or 4 individual 8 cm tartlet tins

Pre-heat the oven to Gas Mark 4/180°C

Pastry:

225 G PLAIN FLOUR	25 G ICING SUGAR
PINCH OF SALT	1 EGG YOLK
140 G BUTTER	COLD WATER TO BIND

- Blend the flour, salt, butter and sugar in a food processor for a few seconds.
- Add enough water to bind it together.
- Turn the pastry out onto a floured surface. Mould the pastry together with your hands, wrap in cling film and chill for 30 minutes.
- Knead the pastry gently and line the chosen tart tin.
- Bake the pastry case, using baking beans, until it has just set (about 10 minutes).
- Remove the baking beans.
- Brush the inside of the pastry case with a little beaten egg white and return to the oven for 2 minutes.

Apple Filling:

350 G BRAMLEY APPLES, PEELED AND CORED	PINCH OF POWDERED CLOVES
120 G CASTER SUGAR	50 G RAISINS
PINCH OF CINNAMON	DESSERTSPOON OF WATER

- Place all the ingredients in a heavy-bottomed saucepan, and simmer slowly until the apples begin to break down.
- Spoon into the baked pastry case.

Meringue:

4 EGG WHITES	PINCH OF SALT	225 G CASTER SUGAR

- Place the egg whites and the pinch of salt into a spotlessly clean bowl.
- Add half the caster sugar and whisk to a soft peak.
- Add the remainder of the sugar and continue to whisk.
- The meringue should be stiff enough to turn upside down and remain in the bowl.
- Pipe decoratively onto the apple.
- Bake until the meringue has set.

APPLE CUSTARD TART

Apple Custard Tart

The competition is to see how many apples you can pile on each tart.
I'll accept nothing less than 2 kg of apples on each tart!

Makes one 9" tart

Pre-heat the oven to Gas Mark 4/180°C

Sweet Pastry:

400 G FLOUR	1 TABLESPOON ICING SUGAR
250 G BUTTER	JUICE OF 1/2 LEMON
1 EGG YOLK	COLD WATER TO BIND

Pastry Cream:

250 ML MILK	50 G CORNFLOUR
2 EGGS	50 G SULTANAS
50 G SUGAR	A SMALL GLASS OF CALVADOS (OPTIONAL)

2 KG OF BRAMLEY APPLES

Bring the milk to the boil.

Whisk the eggs, cornflour and sugar.

Pour on the milk and whisk.

Return to the stove and bring to the boil, stirring continuously.

Stir in the sultanas and a little Calvados.

Allow to cool.

Line a flan ring or a loose bottomed tart tin with the pastry.

Spread with the cold pastry cream.

Top with as many peeled and sliced apples as you can, and sprinkle with sugar.

Bake for 40 minutes until the pastry and the apples are golden.

ORANGE AND
ALMOND CAKE

Orange and Almond Cake

The whole fruit goes into this: skin, pith, flesh and juice, all whizzed up in a food blender to make this squidgy moist pudding cake that is equally good hot or cold. This has been an old faithful on all of my menus, and has recently been discovered at some highly salubrious places! When it's finished in the oven it should be quite wet, and will keep well for days – if you can resist it for that long!

Makes one 8" cake or 1 kg loaf tin

Pre-heat the oven to Gas Mark 4/180°C

3 MEDIUM SIZED ORANGES	6 EGGS
250 G CASTER SUGAR	2 TEASPOONS BAKING POWDER
300 G GROUND ALMONDS	1/2 TEASPOON ALLSPICE

- Wipe the oranges, place in a pot of cold water and bring to the boil.

- Boil for at least 30 minutes: you may need to top up the water occasionally to ensure the oranges are covered.

- Cool the oranges slightly, cut into quarters, remove the pips, and place the whole oranges into a food processor. Purée until smooth.

- Whisk the eggs and the sugar, and add the orange pulp, almonds, baking powder and allspice.

- Pour the batter into a spring-form cake tin or loaf tin and bake for 45 minutes.

- Allow to cool before removing from the tin.

HORLICKS RICE PUDDING

Rice pudding is a personal favourite. I can still recall eating it cold from the tin when enjoying my days off in digs, not wanting to venture into the hotel for fear of getting roped in to some extra veg prep! This is an altogether different affair, with the addition of your Granny's favourite night-cap to give you that warm cosy glow! If you like the skin on the pud, bake it in the oven. If not, simmer it on the stove top, stirring frequently, and it'll be done in half the time.

Serve with ice-cream, blackcurrant jam, grilled cinnamon dusted apples, a tot of whisky – whatever takes your fancy!

Makes 4 portions

Pre-heat the oven to Gas Mark 2/150°C

100 G SHORT GRAIN RICE	1 TABLESPOON HORLICKS
450 ML MILK	40 G BUTTER
450 ML CREAM	FRESHLY GRATED NUTMEG
50 G CASTER SUGAR	

Butter a 1.5 litre (3 pint) pie dish.

Bring the milk and cream to a simmer, and whisk in the Horlicks and sugar.

Place the rice in the pie dish, and pour over the milk mixture.

Grate on the nutmeg and dot on the remaining butter.

Bake for 2 hours.

RHUBARB AND
GINGER CRUMBLE

Rhubarb and Ginger Crumble

In an effort to shed a few pounds, and return to the slim and supple shape of my mid-thirties, I've taken to eating a single bag of sweets every Sunday afternoon. So, sleepless nights have to be endured as I have to pick just one sweet fix for my treat. After much deliberation I've gone for a bumper pack of those strange sours, sometimes apple, sometimes cola. You know the ones: you pop them in and the sides of your mouth retract, your eyes water and your gums melt, before all the sourness melts into a sugary gum. I think this is a throw-back to my early days when we would pick a stick of rhubarb from the garden, steal a packet of sugar and enjoy a dip of sour and sweet! Rhubarb is one of my favourite fruits, even if it is classified as a vegetable! We make jellies, chutneys, poach it with vanilla and sit it on top of coconut waffles, make ice-creams, and even serve it with fish. It's been around in this country since the 1300s, and originates in Asia where it was grown for its medicinal purposes. Legend has it that Generals in the Ming Dynasty would commit suicide drinking a concoction of the leaves and unripe stalks, the oxalic acid being very potent. In many parts of the land it is known as the "pie plant", and as usual, the traditional dishes are invariably the finest. There is little else as classically British as a crumble. Granted, I've spiced it up with ginger and orange, two ingredients which compliment rhubarb wonderfully, and, though it may be just a humble crumble, it's a Great British Crumble!

Serves 4

Pre-heat the oven to Gas Mark 6/200°C

450 G RHUBARB	100 ML GINGER WINE
1 ORANGE, ZEST AND JUICE	200 G CASTER SUGAR
50 G ROOT GINGER, FINELY CHOPPED	

The Crumble:

100 G OATS	150 G CASTER SUGAR
150 G PLAIN FLOUR	125 G BUTTER
25 G TOASTED CHOPPED HAZELNUTS	

- Place the washed chopped rhubarb, the chopped ginger, the sugar and the orange zest in a large saucepan.
- Add the ginger wine and the orange juice.
- Bring the rhubarb to a gentle simmer. Cook gently for 10 minutes, until the rhubarb begins to break up.
- In a mixing bowl, sift the flour and the salt, add the nibbled nuts, the oats and the sugar.
- Using your fingers, rub in the butter until the mixture resembles coarse breadcrumbs.
- Place the rhubarb into a suitable sized pie dish.
- Top with the crumble mixture.
- Sprinkle with caster sugar.
- Bake for 25 minutes.
- Serve with whipped cream, ice-cream or custard.

APRICOT AND
SULTANA COBBLER

Apricot and Sultana Cobbler

Apricots are my favourite autumn fruit, and I can eat scones any time of the day, so this makes pretty much a perfect dish.

Serves 4

Pre-heat the oven to Gas Mark 4/180°C

450 G FRESH APRICOTS	50 G CASTER SUGAR
100 G CASTER SUGAR	65 G BUTTER
50 ML WATER	1 EGG
250 G SELF RAISING FLOUR	75 ML MILK (APPROXIMATELY)
PINCH OF SALT	50 G SULTANAS

Halve and stone the apricots.

Place in an ovenproof dish with the 100 g of caster sugar and the water.

In a mixing bowl combine the flour, salt and sugar.

Add the sultanas.

Rub in the butter.

Add the egg and the milk, gently mixing to make a smooth dough.

Roll out on a floured board until approximately 20 mm thick.

Cut out the scones.

Place the scones on top of the apricots and bake in the oven for 25 minutes.

JAM ROLY POLY

Jam Roly Poly

Whilst steamed sponge, bread and butter pudding and even spotted dick have enjoyed something of a revival, the roly poly seems to have all but disappeared. A great shame!

Serves 4

250 G SELF RAISING FLOUR	140 ML WATER (APPROXIMATELY)
125 G SUET	ZEST OF 1 SMALL ORANGE (OPTIONAL)
PINCH OF SALT	280 G JAM

- Blend the flour, suet, salt and orange zest.
- Bind with the water.
- On a floured board roll into an oblong measuring 300 mm × 250 mm.
- Wet the paste on the edges, and spread with the jam, leaving a 25 mm edge.
- Roll and press the edges to seal.
- Wrap tightly in twice-buttered greaseproof, and steam for 1½ hours.

SUSSEX POND PUDDING

Quite why Sussex should claim this pudding as its own I just don't know. Some people discard the lemon, but a little piece will cut the sweetness of the soaked suet, and the pool of buttery syrup that emerges should be your pond.

Serves 4 people

400 G SELF RAISING FLOUR	PINCH OF SALT
1 TEASPOON BAKING POWDER	1 WHOLE SMALL LEMON
200 G SUET	125 G UNSALTED BUTTER
1 DESSERTSPOON ICING SUGAR	125 G SOFT BROWN SUGAR

1 pudding basin suitable for 4 portions

Prepare a suet pastry by rubbing the suet into the sifted flour, baking powder, sugar and pinch of salt.

Liberally butter the pudding basin.

Line with the pastry, leaving it quite thick (approx 1 cm), and leaving enough for the lid.

Prick the lemon all over with a fork.

Place some of the cubed butter and the sugar in the base of the basin.

Put in the whole lemon.

Add more butter and sugar.

Put on the lid and seal well.

Steam for approximately 3 hours.

Turn out into a deep dish.

TREACLE, APPLE AND
WALNUT TART

Treacle, Apple and Walnut Tart

A creamy treacle tart with the addition of a touch of cream and chopped apples, making it even chewier than usual!

Makes one 22 cm tart

Pre-heat the oven to Gas Mark 6/200°C

Pastry:

50 G BUTTER	150 G PLAIN FLOUR
50 G ICING SUGAR	COLD WATER TO BIND
1 EGG	

- Combine in a food processor, cover and allow to rest for 1 hour.
- Line a 22 cm flan case with the pastry, allowing approximately 3cm overhang.
- Bake blind, covered with baking beans for approximately 15 minutes.
- Remove the parchment and bake for a further 5 minutes.

Filling:

3 EGGS	300 ML DOUBLE CREAM
ZEST AND JUICE OF 1 LEMON	100 G BRIOCHE CRUMBS
1 GRANNY SMITH APPLE	100 G WALNUT PIECES
400 ML GOLDEN SYRUP	

- For the filling, whisk the eggs in a large bowl.
- Add the lemon, apple, syrup and the cream.
- Add the brioche crumbs and the walnuts.
- Mix thoroughly, pour into the pastry case and bake for 40 minutes.

PINEAPPLE UPSIDE
DOWN CAKE

Pineapple Upside Down Cake

Many recipes tell you to use tinned pineapple for this tea-time classic. It will be OK, but I think the fresh pineapple tends to permeate the whole sponge.

Makes one 23 cm cake

Pre-heat the oven to Gas Mark 4/180°C

1 SMALL FRESH PINEAPPLE

225 G CASTER SUGAR

225 G BUTTER

225 G SELF RAISING FLOUR

4 EGGS, BEATEN

Peel and core the pineapple, ensuring you remove all the little eyes from the pineapple outers.

Cream the butter and the sugar.

Gradually add the sifted flour and the beaten eggs to the mixture.

Butter and sprinkle sugar on the base of the cake tin.

Place on the pineapple slices.

Top with the sponge mixture.

Place in the oven for approximately 40 minutes until the sponge is golden brown, checking the centre with a skewer to ensure the centre is cooked.

Turn out onto a wire rack and allow to cool.

MICROWAVE
MARMALADE PUDDING

Microwave Marmalade Pudding

Lots of our pubs are now selling individual sponges which they buy from a frozen food company, reheat in the microwave and then pass off as their own. I really can't see the point in this deception, when they can make one from scratch in the same amount of time! These puddings are to be cooked and served at once – don't try to reheat them!

Serves 4 people

100 G CASTER SUGAR	125 G SELF RAISING FLOUR
2 EGGS	PINCH OF BAKING POWDER
125 G SOFT BUTTER	2 DESSERTSPOONS THICK CUT MARMALADE

- Cream the butter and sugar until light and fluffy.

- Sift the flour and baking powder together.

- Beat the flour and the beaten eggs alternately into the creamed butter and sugar.

- Fold in 1 dessertspoon of marmalade.

- Well butter four cups or large ramekins.

- Divide the remaining spoon of marmalade into the base of the four cups.

- Place the mixture into the cups, filling three-quarters full.

- Place all four cups into the microwave and cook on full power for 60 seconds.

- Turn out and serve immediately.

MINCEMEAT SOUFFLÉ

Mincemeat Soufflé

There is an aura of difficulty surrounding the making of soufflés. They are simple – you just need your guests to be seated and ready as they come from the oven. Spare a thought for Richard Knights in our pastry section: last year we had these on our Christmas Party menu!

Makes 4 individual ramekins

Pre-heat the oven to Gas Mark 6/200°C

150G BEST QUALITY MINCEMEAT	1 WHOLE EGG
200ML MILK	3 EGG YOLKS
40G SUGAR	4 EGG WHITES
25G PLAIN FLOUR	

Heat the milk.

Whisk the egg yolks, whole egg, sugar and flour.

Pour on the milk, stirring continuously.

Return to the heat.

Bring to the boil, stirring continuously.

Remove from the heat, beat in the mincemeat and allow to cool.

Whisk the egg whites to a stiff peak.

Fold through the mixture, taking care not to over mix.

Spoon the mixture into the buttered and sugared ramekins.

Bake in the centre of the oven for about 15 minutes, until the soufflé is well risen.

Serve immediately.

HOT CROSS BUN
AND BUTTER PUDDING

Hot Cross Bun and Butter Pudding

This is a seasonal take on the classic bread and butter pudding – another of these dishes which has been with us for years, but became fashionable overnight when it was featured on a TV programme. The great Anton Mosimann cooked it for a Yorkshire lorry driver and it was hailed a masterpiece! Granted, it's richer using additional egg yolks and cream, and we've used hot cross buns for a lovely warm spicy aroma. You can make it with croissants, brioche, or of course, stale white bread with the crusts off.

A pudding to feed 6-8 people

Pre-heat the oven to Gas Mark 5/190°C

10 HOT CROSS BUNS	½ TEASPOON CINNAMON
4 EGGS	½ VANILLA POD SPLIT
4 EGG YOLKS	CHERRY BRANDY, GRAND MARNIER,
125 G BUTTER	AMORETTO, WHATEVER TAKES YOUR FANCY (OPTIONAL)
500 ML SINGLE CREAM	
100 G CASTER SUGAR	APRICOT JAM AND ICING SUGAR TO GLAZE

- Slice the buns into three, and butter generously.

- Arrange the first layer in a suitable dish. Moisten with a little of your favourite tipple if it's for a special occasion!

- Whisk the eggs and egg yolks with the sugar.

- Bring the cream to the boil with the vanilla pod and cinnamon. Scrape the pod into the cream to disperse the seeds. Simmer for 3 minutes.

- Strain the cream through a fine sieve.

- Whisk onto the eggs and sugar.

- Ladle the custard mixture onto the buns.

- Add another layer of buttered buns and add the remaining custard. Place the dish into a deep tray and add enough hot water to come halfway up the side of the dish. This is known as a water bath or *bain-marie*. Carefully place in the oven. Bake for 45 minutes. The custard should be just set and wobbly.

- Heat a little apricot jam with a little water. Stir.

- Paint the baked pudding with the jam for a lovely shine. Dust with a little icing sugar.

The wow factor!

As any trainee in any hotel kitchen in the world will tell you, the last dish to be served is the most important. Be it the final fry-up for breakfast after a week-long stay, or the afternoon tea before the journey home. In the heady world of the restaurant, it's usually the dessert that makes the final impression. As such, it is an opportunity to show off: perhaps be a little more daring, presuming the diners are sufficiently relaxed, even a little inebriated, so they appreciate a plate with that all-important "wow factor". Nothing thrills us more than when diners gasp with delight, then proceed to take pictures of their puds, sending them to envious friends via their silenced photo phones.

There really is no excuse for the fruit salad/apple pie/gateau option – all it takes is a little imagination and a modicum of effort to finish your meal in style. As such, I've even banished wonderful desserts such as a lemon tart, vanilla crème brûlée and pannacotta, as they seem to appear on every menu that's devoid of a little inspiration and imagination. Not so long ago it was the wobbly sweet trolley that usually sidled up to your table, presenting the remnants of a warm sherry trifle, a collection of pre-packed portions of synthetic cakes, impressively christened gateaux, chewy cheesecakes and the lightest flavourless chemically-compounded creams. Though we blame local government officials for most ills, at least we should congratulate them on their contributions to the demise of the sweet trolley, with the regulatory bodies realising that congealing desserts standing for hours in an evening do little for the constitution, let alone the digestion! I can't put into words how cheated I feel when I am presented with a "bought-in" dessert. It matters little if I've paid £1 or £9: if the kitchen can't be bothered I'll just skip dessert and eat an apple on the way home.

A Revelation from the Oven

Over the past few months I have decided that I really must make an effort to shed a few pounds and return to the slim and supple shape of my mid-thirties. So, out go the crisps, the biscuits and the sweets that all serious chefs seem to live on. Previously I would have a packet of strawberry bon-bons on the dashboard, coconut mushrooms in my coat pocket, and a catering pack of Turkish Delight in the walk-in chiller. Supplement this with a late night supper of Party Rings and Crème Eggs, and you'll see the cause of my chubby chops. I'm often to be found at schools and colleges extolling the virtues of a healthy diet, "five-a-day" and all that, then find myself with a Toffee Crisp for lunch as I head from the classroom straight to the kitchen. I'm still stuck firmly on three sugars in my tea, and can see myself as a fraud, like my old GP who was a forty-a-day man. Every week brings a new determination, that dissipates at the sweet counter as all around me seem to visit the gym as often as they used to visit the pub. Of course I can offer up my excuses, none more so worthy than this book. Collating and baking the recipes we have been assailed with smells, flavours and textures of time gone by. The recipe for the bread pudding, for example, comes straight from the notes in my Mum's *Bero* book. Though she never used a recipe, we faithfully recreated recommendations and the reaction was historic. Everyone who came into the kitchen as it baked remarked on the wonderful smell, as the spices wafted through the extraction system into the car park. Nutmeg is a known hallucinogenic, but I'm sure it is the smell of real baking that puts a grin on everyone's face. We like to consider ourselves trendy and hip when it comes to food, serving Jack Daniels jellies with quail, pea foams with scallops, sugar springs with raspberries, and liquorice ice-cream and the like, but nothing gives as much enjoyment as that simple bread pudding.

BREAD PUDDING

Bread Pudding

This really is a blast from the past. My Mum would always be making this, then it just seemed to disappear from view…and taste! I've never seen it in shops or bakers anywhere. I know it's a poor man's dish – perhaps we've all become a little too posh for our own good. I remember three things quite vividly about this: the crunchy topping, the big fat sultanas, and the residue of fat which would coat the top of your palate when you'd eaten three slabs straight from the pantry!

Pre-heat the oven to Gas Mark 4/180°C

450G WHITE BREAD, PREFERABLY STALE	100G DEMERARA SUGAR
1 PT MILK	2-3 TEASPOONS MIXED SPICE
200G DRIED MIXED FRUIT	2 EGGS
100G CHOPPED PEEL	NUTMEG
100G SUET	

- Remove the crusts and break up the bread.

- Soak in milk for half an hour.

- Beat out any lumps and add all the dried ingredients, except the nutmeg.

- Add the beaten eggs, and a little extra milk if needed.

- Pour in a well-greased tin.

- Grate the nutmeg over the top.

- Bake for 1½-2 hours.

- Dredge with sugar.

SPONGE AND CUSTARD

Sponge and Custard

This is my Mum's standard sponge recipe, which was always a well-received standby. Simply bake the cake mixture in the oven, turn out and serve with lots and lots of custard.

Makes enough for 4, with seconds!

Pre-heat the oven to Gas Mark 4/180°C

250G CASTER SUGAR	4 EGGS
250G BUTTER	100G CURRANTS
250G SELF RAISING FLOUR	

Beat the softened butter with the sugar until pale and creamy.

Add the beaten eggs and the flour, alternately, a little at a time.

Fold in the currants.

Butter a pudding basin or individual moulds.

Place the mixture in, filling the basin about three-quarters full.

Bake for 45 minutes for a large pudding, or 25 minutes for individual bowls.

Seconds, Thirds...
Twelfths!

Every once in a while we open up for Sunday lunch, and for desserts, instead of the spectacular delicate presentation we usually deliver, we'll produce a pudding club table: a white-clothed expanse groaning with all the classics. Accompanying these heavyweights we will have jam sauce, fresh cream, chocolate sauce, golden syrup, syllabubs, butterscotch, and the matriarch of them all – jugs upon jugs of custard. Everyone expects it, everyone wants it, everyone, it seems, loves it. The waddling diner can visit the table as many times as they wish, the only rule to be a member of the pudding club...a clean plate before you can return for seconds, thirds or fourths. Last year we had one delicate lady who appeared over a dozen times! I am a veteran of such lunches, but new members of the kitchen brigade always enquire how much custard they need to make: four pints, five pints? Make it gallons I say in all seriousness! I abhor these carvery lunches where you queue to get in, queue to get your food, queue to pay. I know the English are renowned for their restraint whilst queuing for a bus, but for Sunday lunch? Part of the attraction seems to be the attempt to pile as much food onto a small plate as is humanly possible. Then, balancing like a circus performer, you have to get the plate back to your table without spilling gravy down your front. Having spent three years working in just such a place, I swore I'd never go down this route in my restaurant. Having seen the success of our pudding club table, perhaps I should shelve my snobbishness and relent.

Custard Forever

Custard: the sign of a serious pudding! This thick yellow confection is an institution, beloved of gentlemen's clubs, public schools, council estates, gourmets and gluttons. No food invokes memories, inspires greed, and reflects personalities like custard. Thick, thin, hot or cold, with skin, it matters little…or it's the biggest issue in life.

The French realise our devotion, christening real custard "sauce anglais". Real custard, according to the aficionados, consists of egg yolks, sugar, milk and vanilla, but to households across the country, *real* custard means fresh milk thickened with Bird's custard powder. Ask any Brit aboard what they miss about this country, and invariably it's Bird's custard and Branston pickle! Whenever I have a customer, usually an elderly gentleman, who asks for real custard, I know he's looking for Bird's! As an arrogant, egotistical, know-all chef, I'm not allowed cornflour custard in my restaurant kitchen, but a peek in my home kitchen will reveal the distinctive tin, ready for my Sunday afters.

Today, it would seem we are even too busy to make this treat, and you can buy pots of ready-made fresh custard, but this sickly lazy-sod concoction bears no resemblance to "fresh" powder custard straight from the tin! When a chef pâtissier makes custard he will give you something different: a kind of hybrid, still with eggs, milk, sugar and vanilla, but thickened with flour to give a delicious filling for choux buns, mille feuille, or used as a base for soufflés. Known as "crème pâtisserie" or confectioner's custard this is delicious, but it ain't custard! If you really are too busy to make a pudding, at least give them a bowl of custard – you might just get away with it!

"Please may I have some more, Mum"

Custard

*This is a very grand recipe for custard for special occasions, but if you want the stuff of your childhood,
simply follow the instructions on the back of the tin!*

6 EGG YOLKS	**250** ML WHIPPING CREAM
100 G CASTER SUGAR	VANILLA POD

- Bring the cream to the boil with the vanilla pod, then turn down and simmer for 5 minutes.

- Whisk the egg yolks and the sugar until pale.

- Pour the cream on to the yolks, stirring continuously.

- Return to a low heat, and continue to stir until the mixture begins to thicken.

- Do not allow the mixture to boil: you'll end up with a vanilla scrambled egg!

- Serve with sponge, crumble, roly poly, stewed prunes – anything and everything.

THE WINES OF THE GREATEST WINE
MAKER IN THE WORLD, WILLI OPITZ

Enjoying Dessert Wines with your Pudding

The greatest dessert wines are rich, flavoursome and beautifully textured, counterbalanced by a wonderful, cleansing freshness. In what can often be a dull world, they offer a lingering moment of hedonism – and they can partner many foods other than desserts. However, all devotees of the pudding course should certainly explore the variety of dessert wines available: nothing else rounds off a dinner party to greater effect. The key to appreciating the many different styles of these wines is to understand how their increased sugar content is achieved.

In many cases, it is down to a most peculiar phenomenon known as Noble Rot. Most winemakers go out of their way to protect their grapes from rot, yet in some wine regions of the world it is positively encouraged. The micro-organism that these winemakers seek is *Botrytis cinerea*, a yeast which thrives when there are damp, misty mornings followed by warm sun-baked afternoons. For this reason, almost all "botrytised" wines originate from vineyards close to lakes or rivers. Two famous examples are Sauternes (from Bordeaux, around the confluence of the *Ciron* and *Garonne* rivers) and Tokay (from Hungary, alongside the *Bodrog*). There are many others, including the sweet wines of the Loire Valley in France and the great *Beerenausleses* and *Trockenbeerenausleses* of Germany and Austria.

The Noble Rot organism colonises the skin of the grapes, puncturing them. The damaged grapes consequently dehydrate, increasing the concentration of the sugar present. Such grapes look terrible: shrivelled and peppered with mould. But, by a seemingly miraculous process, they produce beautifully pure, rich, sweet and golden wines. Flavours of apricots, peaches and honey abound – originating as much from the botrytis as from the grapes.

Few wine regions are blessed with the conditions that favour Noble Rot, and yet many manage to produce excellent dessert wines. Another way to achieve the desired sugar concentration is to leave the grapes on the vines, long after the normal harvest time in September. Delaying the picking causes a gradual dehydration of the grapes, resulting in sweet wines of great depth and complexity of flavour. 'Late harvest' wines can be found in wine regions the world over, but particularly enjoyable examples come from Alsace (where they are labelled *Vendanges Tardives*), from Jurançon in south-west France and from Constantia in South Africa.

The ultimate late harvest wine is Eiswein, translating literally as 'ice wine'. These examples are produced from grapes left to hang until frozen, eventually being picked by frost-bitten fingers in the depths of winter. Already dehydrated, the grapes also lose water through being frozen, concentrating the sugar content even further. It is a style which once was unique to Germany, but there are now fantastic examples from Austria and Canada too.

Undoubtedly, the very greatest dessert wines are produced from dehydrated grapes, often as a result of Noble Rot. But excellent dessert wines can be produced by other methods. In some cases, fermentation may be arrested by the addition of spirit – the unfermented sugars provide the sweetness, whilst the added spirit bumps up the alcohol content. This is how the French *Vin Doux Naturel* wines are produced, the most well-known example probably being Muscat de Beaumes de Venise.

There are many other such wines, particularly from around Roussillon and the Languedoc, and also from Australia. Finally, there are certain grape varieties that yield massive amounts of sugar and are naturally still sweet when fully fermented. One such variety is Pedro Ximénez, the basis of all sweet Sherry.

A glass of dessert wine makes an excellent match for many types of food, not just puddings. Late harvest wines or Sauternes will complement beautifully a starter of foie gras, or the great ewe's milk cheese of Roquefort.

But it is with the final course that the dessert wine really comes into its own. Fruit-based puddings, particularly where autumn and stone fruits are concerned, match well with the apricot and apple flavours found in botrytised wine, such as Sauternes. Summer fruits and meringues are more likely to meet their perfect companion in a Muscat, either a *Vendange Tardives* style from Alsace or a Muscat de Beaumes de Venise. Puddings featuring almonds, or other nuts, are best paired with Sauternes. Cheesecake needs something with good acidity to cut through the richness; so look to Germany or the Loire Valley. Chocolate puddings are the most recalcitrant: consider a Tokay, but the best option may well be a fortified Australian Muscat.

Always serve the wine chilled, in a white wine glass, but otherwise there are no rules. Simply relax and enjoy some of the world's greatest wines in the perfect setting – matched with a great pudding!

Trevor Hughes
T & W Wines Ltd
5 Station Way
Brandon
Suffolk
IP27 0BH

Tel: 01842 814414
Fax: 01842 819967
contact@tw-wines.com
www.tw-wines.com

Index

Notes and Comments